ART FROM WOOD

with projects using branches, leaves, and seeds

Gillian Chapman & Pam Robson

Thomson Learning

New York

SALVAGED!

Art from Fabric
Art from Packaging
Art from Paper
Art from Rocks and Shells
Art from Sand and Earth
Art from Wood

First published in the United States in 1995 by
Thomson Learning
115 Fifth Avenue
New York, NY 10003

Published simultaneously in Great Britain
by Wayland (Publishers) Limited

Library of Congress Cataloging-in-Publication
Chapman, Gillian.
    Art from wood : with projects using branches, leaves,
and seeds / Gillian Chapman & Pam Robson.
        p.   cm.—(Salvaged!)
    Includes bibliographical references and index.
    ISBN 1-56847-383-4
    1. Nature craft—Juvenile literature. 2. Collage (Art)—
Juvenile literature. 3. Assemblage (Art)—Juvenile literature.
4. Wood in art—Juvenile literature. [1. Nature craft.
2. Handicraft.] I. Robson, Pam. II. Title. III. Series.
TT910.C48   1995
745.5—dc20   94-43233

Printed in Italy

Acknowledgments
Special thanks to K.C. for his help in making the projects.
Photographs on p. 4: Robert Harding,
on p. 5: top Tony Stone/Sister Daniel,
and on p. 5: inset The Grizedale Society.

Contents

Our Precious Forests

Deforestation

Forests are a vital part of the global ecosystem and home to millions of species of animals and plants. Millions of trees are cut down for timber or to provide land for growing crops or grazing animals. Their destruction causes ecological harm and may contribute to climate changes. Deforestation is one of the many environmental problems that could threaten the future of our planet.

Rain forests are disappearing at a tremendous rate every day.

Agenda 21

In 1992, world leaders met in Rio de Janeiro for an Earth Summit. Together they approved a plan, Agenda 21, to help save the planet's trees. The tree of life is the plan's symbol. Trees are the lungs of our planet, yet nearly thirty square miles of rain forest are destroyed every hour. Agenda 21 asks people to slow this rate by using trees that would normally be discarded and by reusing old timber.

A Wasteful Society

We live in a society that wastes the Earth's limited natural resources. This book suggests ideas for recycling old wood and tree litter. These projects show beautiful ways to use forests without destroying them.

The Tree of Life

In ancient times, trees were worshipped as a source of power. People believed that by using bark and foliage, the spirit of the trees could be captured. The tree of life, an image of a tree, is featured in the folk art of many cultures, particularly that of Mexico. In West Africa, some flags carry tree-of-life images.

A deer sculpture made from twigs by Sophie Ryder stands in a forest in northern England.

Greek Mythology

The ancient Greeks believed that trees were inhabited by their gods. Wood nymphs, or dryads—the daughters of Zeus—were said to come to life with each new tree and, eventually, to die with it.

Ancient Trees

Tree life spans vary according to each species. Some trees are more than 4,000 years old and centuries of history—from fires to droughts—are now recorded in their growth rings. Trees support ecosystems of flora and fauna that have survived for generations.

Materials from Trees

Trees provide food, fuel, and shade. They act as windbreaks and hold the soil, preventing erosion. From trees we get wood to make paper, rubber, cork, and kapok. Many vital medicines come from trees. Perhaps most importantly, trees transpire. That means they take in carbon dioxide and send oxygen into the air. People and animals breathe in oxygen.

Storm Damage

Storm winds can devastate forests and woods—hurricanes can uproot trees. Storm-damaged wood is often left to rot or it is burned. Such materials can be used for projects in this book.

Tree Litter

Trees constantly shed bark, leaves, fruits, or seeds. Healthy seeds mean more trees will grow. One useful project you can do is plant a tree.

Pattern and Texture

Design in Nature

Forests are a source of inspiration to artists, scientists, and people who love nature. In them we find harmony of shape and design. Forests are full of patterns and perfect proportions—look closely at the form of a pine cone or a leaf.

Observing and Collecting

Collect leaves, seeds, and pieces of wood and bark from the forest floor. Look at their lines, patterns, and shapes; feel the different textures. Do the lines on a piece of bark look like ripples on water?

Arrange your collection in simple patterns, according to shape and color. Use a flat surface for your pattern making. Working outdoors can be inspiring.

Natural materials for projects

Withered and preserved leaves

Preserving Materials

Natural materials begin to wither and decay once they fall from the trees. Seeds, bark, and pieces of wood last longer if they are stored in a cool, dry place.

Leaves will start to lose their color immediately. Coating them in melted, but not boiling, wax will help them to keep their color. You can stand bunches of leaves and grasses in a silica gel. This dries the plants so they won't rot, but they will lose some of their color. You can buy silica gel in most craft stores.

Seasonal Materials

Natural materials are seasonal. That means they are found only at certain times of the year. Leaves can only be collected during autumn, or, in the tropics, during the dry season. In the temperate regions of the southern hemisphere, it is autumn when the north is having its spring. In the tropics there are two seasons—wet and dry. The weather affects all natural materials. Collect them on dry, sunny days from the ground around the tree. Do not break anything from a living tree.

Simple patterns using natural materials

Temporary Patterns

Craftspeople have always made patterns using natural materials. These simple works of art are often of a spiritual nature and are meant to be temporary. Today, many artists carry on this tradition and place their artwork in a chosen environment where it is left to be blown away by the wind and rain—the only record possibly being a photograph. You can take photographs of your leaf and seed patterns to keep as a record.

Pictures in Frames

Collage Shapes

Color, pattern, and texture play an important part in the design of a collage. The natural materials may suggest a picture. Look carefully at all the objects in your tree litter collection. Do any of them have shapes that suggest something to you? Sycamore seeds may remind you of a pair of ears. Some leaves make hand shapes. Look at the rooster's tail in the collage below. Plan your design first. Sketch it on a sheet of paper or draw directly onto the backing on which you'll glue the material.

Collage Pictures

Collage work should be stuck onto a rigid surface. Your design may look better on a colored or textured background. Before gluing anything down, move your materials around to find the best arrangement. White glue is best for lightweight materials such as leaves, twigs, and seeds. A diluted solution of white glue and water will make a glaze that can be applied to the finished collage. This will help preserve the natural materials so they do not decay.

Plan your design first

Rooster collage

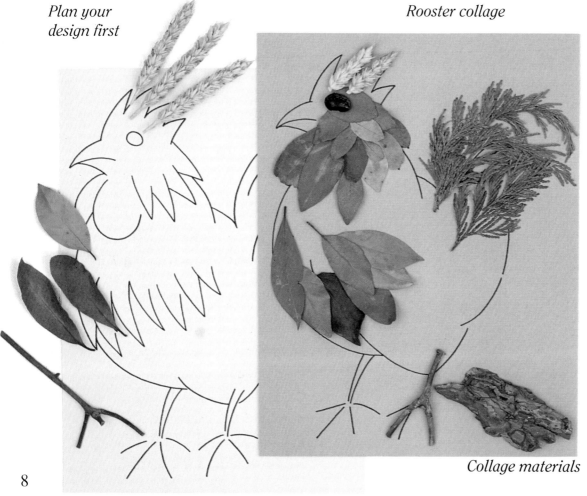

Collage materials

Collages and frames

Natural Glues

Whenever possible use water-based, environmentally friendly glues. In the forests you can see examples of natural glues. Pine trees produce a sticky sap to protect damaged branches. This sap eventually becomes amber and often contains the bodies of trapped insects. Spiders build sticky webs as food traps. Wasps' nests are held together with a papier-mâché-like substance the wasps create from chewed wood.

Making a Picture Frame

A collage will look nice in a natural frame. Make a frame from cardboard, cutting out a window slightly smaller than the picture. The frame should cover the rough edges of the collage. Cut a piece of cardboard to use as backing. It should be bigger than the picture, but smaller than the outside of the frame. Put the frame over the picture. Glue the backing to the frame behind the picture. You can decorate the frame with other objects. Hang your collage on the wall.

Collage Walks

All the materials you need to make natural collages are freely available. In towns and cities, you can look in parks and gardens—even on grass borders. In the countryside, you can look in hedges and woods. Here are some ideas for displaying and recording the finds of a nature walk.

Footprint Collage

This is a collage of materials found underfoot while walking through a park or forest. All kinds of interesting leaves, twigs, and seeds—and even litter—make up the collage. Draw a large human or animal footprint on stiff cardboard. Arrange your materials in the shape. When you are pleased with the design, glue everything down.

Footprint collage

Walk in time

The scale along the bottom records each minute of the walk.

10

Walk in Time

If you are planning a long walk through a forest or park, make a record of your progress as you collect materials. Keep a note of the time, the weather, and the type of countryside through which you are walking. When you get home, arrange your collection on a horizontal strip of cardboard with your notes. You could sketch or paint the landscape as a background for the collage.

Long Walks

You may also arrange your collection on a vertical strip. Glue or sew each item on paper or fabric, arranging them in the order in which you found them. The natural changes in the countryside you walked through will be apparent by the items collected.

When you are walking in the countryside, think about why you are attracted to certain materials. What makes you pick up one leaf or stone and not another similar one? Is it a particular shape or color that appeals to you? When you are sorting and cleaning the materials at home, you will use some, but discard others. Think about why you make your choices.

Long walks

Found Objects

Sculpture from Found Objects

An artist using found objects to create works of art is a collector and creator. Found art describes art created almost entirely from objects found in nature. The artist is guided by the natural shape of these objects. While you are walking in the woods or along a beach, look for interesting pieces of wood. Do the shapes suggest anything to you? A branch may have a texture that resembles animal fur. A piece of wood may have a strange, weathered shape. You could also smooth pieces of wood with sandpaper and carve them into other shapes.

Driftwood snakes

Bark jigsaw

Bark Jigsaws

Tree bark is a hard, protective layer of dead tissue. As a tree grows, the bark around the trunk cracks and becomes deeply furrowed. Each species of tree has its own distinctive bark pattern. Some trees shed their bark and this can be collected. Never strip bark from a living tree or the tree will die. Bark comes in a variety of colors, textures, and thicknesses. Look around the foot of a pine tree. You may find some bark sections. Try matching them up to create a bark jigsaw.

Branch collage

Branch Collage

Ask an adult to saw a small branch into cross sections. Observe the growth rings inside each section. Arrange the pieces on a wooden background to make a branch collage.

Joining bundles of twigs

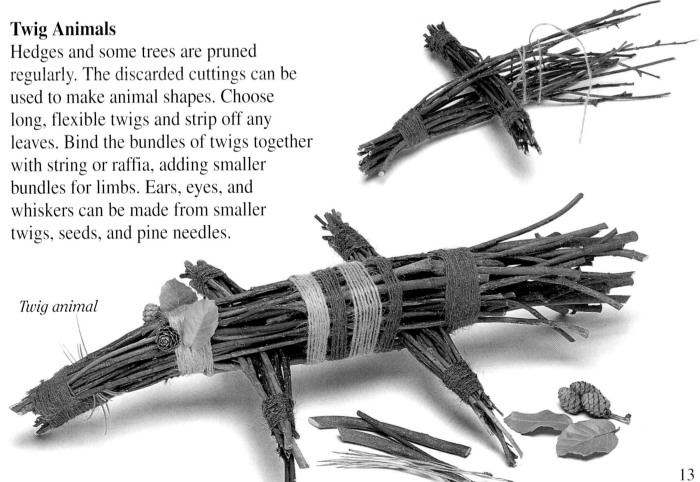

Twig Animals

Hedges and some trees are pruned regularly. The discarded cuttings can be used to make animal shapes. Choose long, flexible twigs and strip off any leaves. Bind the bundles of twigs together with string or raffia, adding smaller bundles for limbs. Ears, eyes, and whiskers can be made from smaller twigs, seeds, and pine needles.

Twig animal

13

Tools to Make Marks

Ancient Crafts

The first simple tools may have been sticks found among tree litter. The Aboriginal dreamtime story pictures were first recorded on bark and stone using sticks and fibers as tools. The ends were frayed or had hairs or feathers attached. American Indians in the southwest softened the ends of yucca stalks by chewing—the stalks were used as brushes to paint pottery.

Tools for Working

Look in tree litter for twigs and dried seed heads to use as pattern-making tools. Make brushes by tying dried grasses, feathers, or pine needles to twigs. Push thistle heads into hollowed elderberry wood handles. Experiment with a range of natural materials. Each will make a different mark. Cut a design into the cross section of a twig. Look for sticks of charcoal in a burned-out bonfire and try drawing with them.

dried grasses

dried seed head

squashed twig

pine needles

feathers

charcoal

Brushes and the marks they make

Bark painting

Stone painting

Surfaces to Work On

Early peoples worked on bark and foliage in the belief that the power of the tree then passed to them. The Fijians made a bark cloth called tapa on which patterns were stamped with leaves and bamboo tubes dipped in dye. The Aztecs made paper from bark. Use your handmade brushes to make patterns on stone and bark.

Natural Pigments

Charcoal powder and natural pigments of ground ocher and clay were probably used to create the famous stone age cave paintings of spotted horses found at Pech-Merle in France.

Charcoal is made by burning wood inside a container that only lets a little air in. The best kind of wood is obtained by coppicing trees. This involves clearing a small area within a forest, allowing sunlight to enter and letting young trees grow. Coppicing is good for the environment because it encourages ecosystems to thrive.

Twig Tool Container

Make a twig container to store your tools by cutting down a plastic bottle and covering it with twigs. Hold the twigs in place with tape while working, but bind them together with string to finish.

Printing sticks

Twig tool container

15

Rubbings and Stencils

Tree Types

A tree can be identified by its bark. Bark is the tree's armor against the elements. It protects the living tissue beneath from the weather, insects, and even fire. It is found in an amazing variety of colors and textures. Some insects bore into the bark and create distinctive marks. As strips of old bark peel off, new bark is revealed growing underneath. On a giant sequoia the bark may be up to a foot thick.

Making a leaf rubbing

Book of rubbings

Bark and Leaf Rubbings

By taking bark rubbings from a wide variety of trees, you can learn a lot about textures. You may also choose leaves that have a distinctive shape and prominent veins. Make your rubbing with a wax crayon. Place a sheet of light-colored paper over the reverse side of a leaf. Rub gently with a crayon. The image of the leaf will appear. Take bark and leaf rubbings from the same tree and make a book to keep a record of your best rubbings. Label and date your work, putting bark and leaf rubbings from the same tree together.

Natural Templates

Leaves come in so many shapes and sizes that they make perfect natural templates for stenciling and splatter pictures. Choose strong leaves that have a bold shape—sycamore, maple, and oak leaves are ideal. Ferns and grasses are interesting, but are too delicate to use.

Splatter Painting

Dip an old toothbrush or nailbrush in paint and stroke the bristles with a stick to make the paint splatter over the leaf stencil. Practice on scrap paper before you start a project. Be careful not to let the paint get too watery. Build your design by overlapping the leaf shapes and changing the paint color. Let each layer of paint dry before adding another, to avoid smudges.

Splatter scroll

Splatter Scrolls and Lanterns

Make a series of splatter leaf patterns on a long piece of paper or fabric. You can turn it into a hanging scroll or banner. Attach branches to each end of the scroll. Hang it with string.

Paper decorated with leaf splatter patterns can be curled around a glass jar containing a candle. The candle will glow through the printed paper, showing the leaf pattern. This makes a good Halloween lantern. Get an adult's permission to do this project, and never leave a burning candle unattended.

Splatter lanterns

17

Natural Block Prints

Woodcuts

In the fifteenth and sixteenth centuries woodcut illustrations became popular in Germany. A design was drawn onto a wood block. Some parts were cut away, leaving the design in relief. Early wood blocks were made from softwood like pear or beech. The block was cut along the wood grain so little detail was possible. Later, wood engravers used hardwood blocks cut across the grain, and more delicate lines could be cut.

Printing papers

Making Natural Blocks

Instead of carving a design, you can glue a raised pattern onto a wood block. Interesting shapes like leaves, grasses, and evergreen twigs are ideal materials. Cut blocks of wood from discarded branches. Glue foliage to the flat surface. Apply paint to the raised design with a brush or roller, then press the block onto paper. Practice on scrap paper before starting on a large piece of work.

Seasoned Wood Blocks

Wood from the forest floor contains moisture that makes it weaker and less elastic. Wood from a lumberyard has been seasoned, or dried out, making it stronger. Use scraps of seasoned wood to make blocks. Create relief patterns with scraps of dowel, used matchsticks, and other small objects.

Printing blocks

Using Your Prints

The advantage of a printing block is that a design can be made and repeated for as long as the block lasts. Blocks are ideal for creating exciting patterns and effects that have many practical applications.

Experiment by painting your printing blocks with different colors and alternating and reversing the blocks for a range of patterns. The finished printed papers can be used as wrapping paper to cover presents or gift boxes.

A single design that works well, such as an individual leaf or fern motif, can be used to decorate writing paper, labels, and envelopes.

Printed papers can also be used to cover and protect books and folders, making them unique.

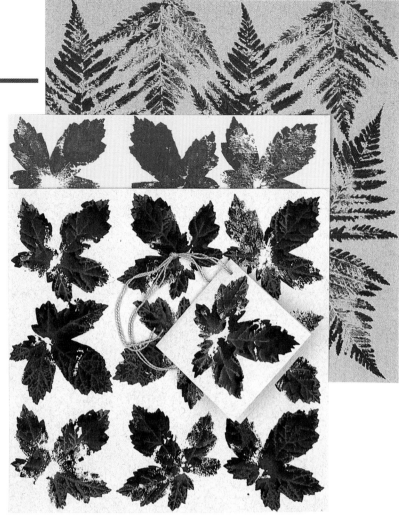

Printed giftwrap

Writing paper

Envelope and label

Giftbox and tag

19

Knots and Branches

Wood

Wood is an organic material; it comes from a living tree and has many uses. There are two main types of trees—softwoods such as pine, and hardwoods such as mahogany. Hardwoods take many years to grow to full size.

Willow and yew can be used for basket weaving. Sycamore can be carved. Sailing ships like the *Mayflower* were built from oak. The color of each wood varies—pine looks very different from mahogany. Look for the knots in wooden furniture.

Polished wood showing knots and grain

Knots

The side branches of a tree make small ring-like markings in the wood. These can only be seen when the wood is cut into plank sections. When you visit a carpenter's workshop or a lumberyard look at a variety of seasoned wood planks and observe the knot patterns. Recreate these patterns by drawing knot designs or try taking rubbings of knots in wood. Furniture makers use the knot patterns in wood to make furniture more attractive.

Knotting Threads

Whenever you use string or thread in craftwork, you will need to tie it with a secure knot. These diagrams show you how to tie some very useful knots.

How to tie knots

clove hitch

slip knot

reef knot

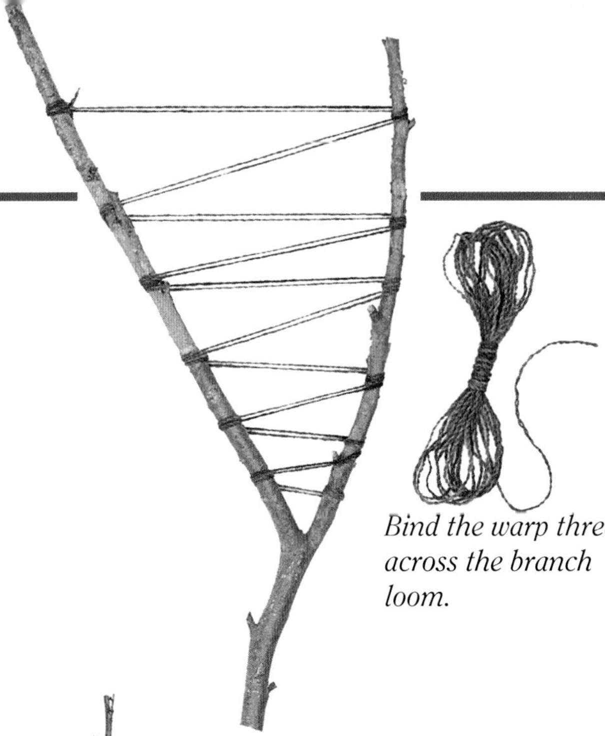

Branch Weaving

Branch weaving is an easy introduction to the techniques of weaving. A forked branch acts as a simple loom when threads are bound across. Grasses, leaves, feathers, and other natural materials can be woven through the threads at random.

Bind the warp thread across the branch loom.

Choosing Materials

The success of the finished weaving will depend on the choice of the branch loom. At first, a branch with two or three forks is enough. Other branches should be cut off. Tie a length of string or colored yarn to the top fork and wind it back and forth across the branch, as shown in the diagram. These are the warp threads. Natural materials can now be woven in and out through these threads—over one strand and under the next.

As you get more confident you can experiment with more complex branch looms, threading all kinds of materials into the weaving.

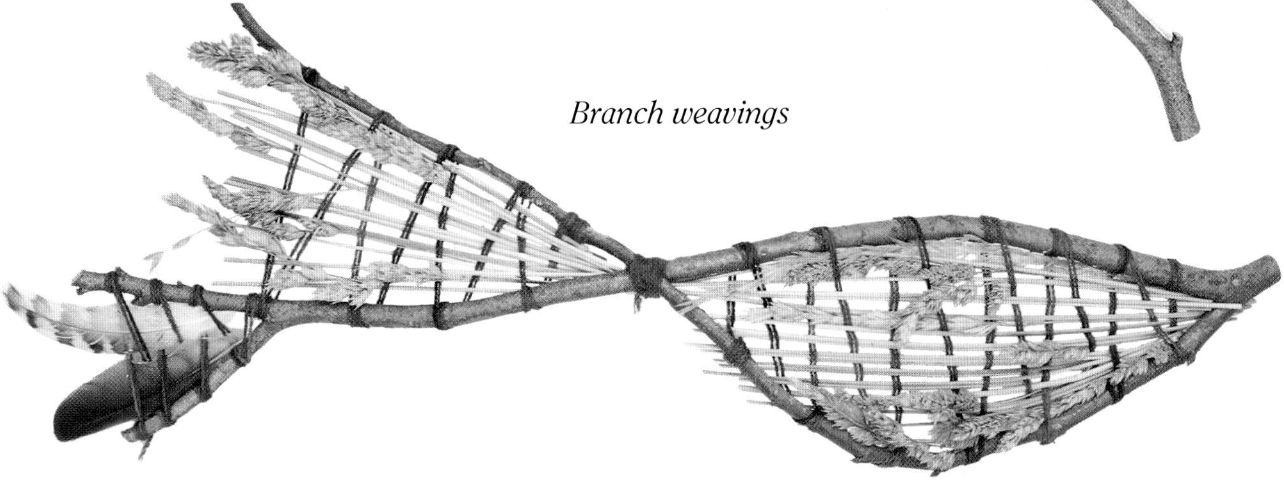

Branch weavings

Wall Hangings

Weaving from Natural Materials

With natural materials from forests and woods you can create attractive designs.

The North American Indians of the northwest coast relied on materials from the red cedar tree for their homes, clothing, and artifacts. They were able to weave waterproof cloth from bark.

During World War II, when supplies of cotton were cut off, the Germans used nettle fibers to weave sandbags for the army. Nettle cloth weaving is used in Nepal today.

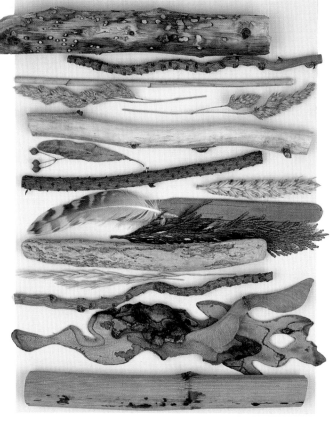

Lay the materials out on scrap paper first.

Making a loom

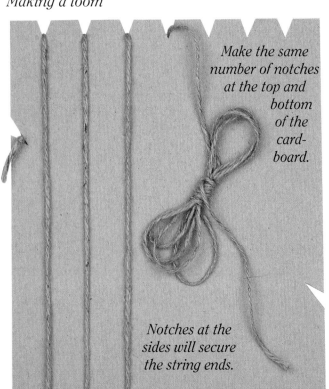

Make the same number of notches at the top and bottom of the cardboard.

Notches at the sides will secure the string ends.

Planning and Sorting

Making a weaving can be a small individual project or the result of a group working together. Because you are using natural materials the finished weaving will be of a temporary nature. Try not to use fresh materials that will shrivel quickly, like green leaves. Choose dry grasses, twigs, seeds, and feathers that will last longer.

Sort your natural materials according to texture and color. Lay them out first on scrap paper, making sure you have plenty to choose from. Plan your design, making it interesting and surprising. Include any unusual items you find.

Weaving Materials

Weave long flexible twigs and grasses in and out of the warp threads. Fill in the gaps between thicker pieces of wood with woven string and grasses to help support them. Try to start and finish with a strong piece of wood that stretches across the weaving.

Removing the Loom

When the weaving is complete you will need to take it off the cardboard. Cut the warp threads halfway down the cardboard at the back, two or three at a time. Knot them together at the top and bottom and cut off the excess string. Continue until all the threads are knotted. Hang the weaving by the top threads. Try tying pebbles to the bottom threads to make weighted tassels, decorated with seeds and grasses.

Making a Loom

For most weavings you can use a cardboard loom. Cut a piece of strong cardboard the same size as your design. Make notches along two opposite sides and wind string around them forming the warp threads. Secure both ends of the string very firmly because the weaving will be under a lot of tension when you begin working.

Weaving in progress

Wall hanging

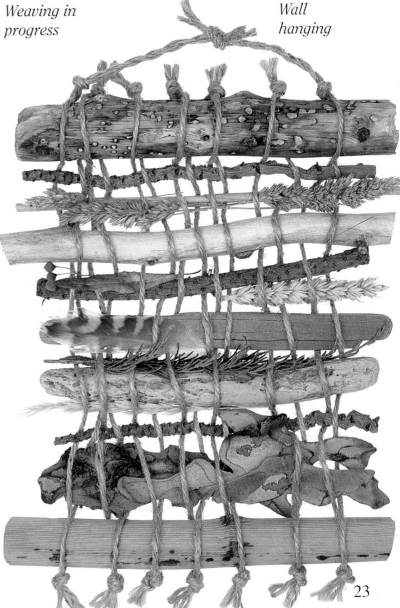

23

Leaf Baskets

Why Do Leaves Change Color?

Deciduous trees shed their leaves in autumn so the trees can survive the winter by conserving water. The green of the leaves is caused by the presence of chlorophyll. As the chlorophyll begins to disappear, the sugars in the leaves create new red, orange, and yellow colors.

Leaf Litter

Trees are constantly shedding litter. Leaf litter is the organic matter found on the forest floor. Mixed with the dead leaves are twigs, bark, fruits, seeds, and other natural materials. Gradually leaf litter decomposes as it reacts with water, air, and minerals to form a layer of new soil. Trees make their own soil by dropping leaves, branches, and bark onto the forest floor. This soil provides the necessary nutrients for new trees to grow.

Growing Trees in Leaf Pots

By growing trees from seeds and transplanting the saplings in the right environment, you are helping to preserve the growing cycle. Collect healthy seeds from the forest floor and grow them in leaf pots. Make the leaf pots in the same way as the leaf baskets opposite using plastic flower pots as molds. When your saplings are strong enough, find suitable places to transplant them in their leaf pots. They could grow throughout your lifetime.

Coppicing

New growth also needs sunlight. Coppicing not only provides the raw materials for charcoal and other wood products but also allows sunshine to enter dense woods. In this way new ecosystems are encouraged to develop.

Tree saplings growing in leaf pots

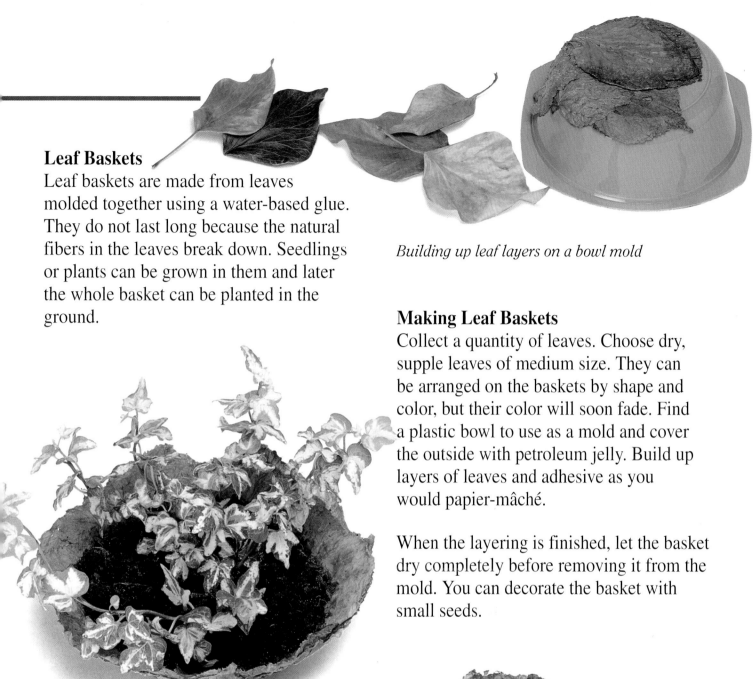

Leaf Baskets

Leaf baskets are made from leaves molded together using a water-based glue. They do not last long because the natural fibers in the leaves break down. Seedlings or plants can be grown in them and later the whole basket can be planted in the ground.

Building up leaf layers on a bowl mold

Making Leaf Baskets

Collect a quantity of leaves. Choose dry, supple leaves of medium size. They can be arranged on the baskets by shape and color, but their color will soon fade. Find a plastic bowl to use as a mold and cover the outside with petroleum jelly. Build up layers of leaves and adhesive as you would papier-mâché.

When the layering is finished, let the basket dry completely before removing it from the mold. You can decorate the basket with small seeds.

Leaf baskets

Animal Houses

Ecosystems

Trees are vital to the survival of forest and woodland ecosystems. Around an oak tree, there is a tightly knit community of plants and animals that rely upon each other for survival. Established food chains exist. Oak moth caterpillars eat the leaves, small birds eat the caterpillars, sparrow hawks eat the small birds. In the tree, squirrels eat the acorns and on the ground other tiny mammals feed on the leaf litter.

In tropical rain forests, even more complex ecosystems exist. These disappear daily as huge areas of the forests are destroyed.

How to Make an Animal House

Making an animal house is not as difficult as it seems but you will need an adult to help you use tools like the drill and hammer. Collect all the scraps of wood you can find.

A rough plan for the animal house is outlined here but you may need to adapt it to suit the materials you have. Design the house with a particular creature in mind. It might be a nesting box for wild birds or a home for a pet mouse or a hamster. Any sawdust and wood shavings can be kept as bedding material for small animals and birds.

Construction plan

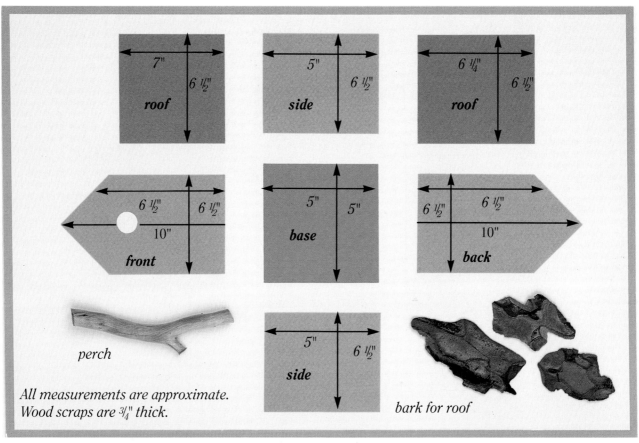

All measurements are approximate. Wood scraps are ¾" thick.

Planning the Construction

Using wood, construct a basic box shape with a sloping roof. It will help if you make a plan of the house first. Measure and mark the wood carefully according to your plan. Then get an adult to cut it with a saw.

Arrange all the pieces, making sure they will fit exactly. The entrance must be cut to an appropriate size. To suit small birds like titmice, ask an adult to drill the entrance hole in the front piece using a hand drill with a bit about one inch wide. Make it larger to encourage bigger visitors. If used for mice or hamsters, cut a hole near the bottom of the front piece.

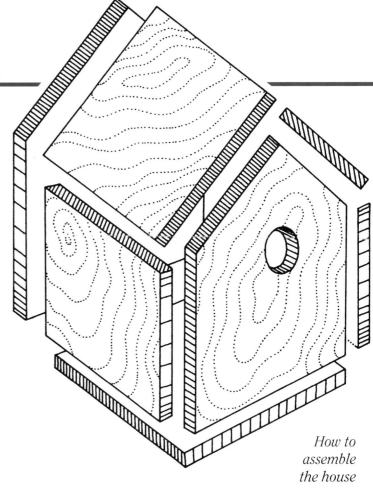

How to assemble the house

Begin by nailing the sides to the front and back. Attach the base with screws so you can remove it to clean the house yearly if it is being used for birds. Nail on the roof sections. Use small tacks and be careful with the hammer! One roof section is larger than the other. Overlap them for a neat finish.

Finishing off

Decorate the roof with pieces of bark. Nail a twig perch outside the entrance hole if it is for birds. Make the house weatherproof by coating it with varnish.

Animal house

Making Music

Early Music

The first musical instruments were made from wood. Wood is a resonant material through which sound vibrations can travel. The Kwilu River people of Africa created a humming drum by piercing the membrane covering the wooden body of the drum with a stick. The drummer would use a handful of wet leaves to grasp the stick inside the hollow body and slide his hand up and down to make the sound.

The Ancient Greeks had huge rowing boats called triremes. To help the rowers keep in time, a musician played two pipes made out of wood. The pipes were known as auloi and the musician was the aulete.

Panpipes

Bind the pipes to the bamboo supports.

The Legend of Panpipes

Pan, the Greek god of shepherds, had the horns, ears, and legs of a goat. He fell in love with the nymph, Syrinx, but she did not love him. Taking pity on Syrinx, the gods changed her into a reed. Pan cut a reed and made it into a pipe in memory of his lost love. Panpipes are traditional folk instruments still played in China, Latin America, Europe, and especially Romania. Recently, archaeologists discovered a set of Roman boxwood panpipes in London.

Making Panpipes

These panpipes are made from lengths of bamboo. Cut a six-inch length of bamboo, with one end open, as shown here. Cut a notch in the bamboo about $1\frac{1}{4}$" from the open end. Plug the same end with a section of wood. Blow into the pipe and move the plug in and out until you have the best sound, then glue the plug in place. Make a set of pipes of different lengths and bind them together.

Cutting the bamboo

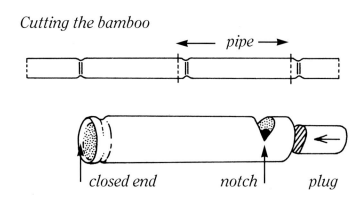

closed end   *notch*   *plug*

Rattles and Rasps

A rattle can be made by making holes in walnut shells and threading them onto a loop of wire. Alternatively, fill hollow gourds or coconuts with different seeds. Small, light seeds give soft, whispery sounds. Heavier seeds and pods give a stronger rattle. A rasp is a wooden instrument in which grooves have been cut. Sticks are passed over the grooves, making a rhythmic sound. Cut grooves in a piece of wood and make your own rasp.

Walnut rattle

Rasp and stick

Drumsticks

Drums and Xylophones

Banging one piece of wood with another must have made the first rhythmic sounds. Make a collection of branches and logs of various sizes and listen to the range of sounds that can be made by drumming them together. Can you create different notes? Does one wood make a higher sound than another? When you have experimented, make a xylophone with a range of notes. The sticks used to bang the instruments will also affect the sound. Try making a series of drumsticks using different materials.

Driftwood xylophone

29

Glossary

amber A fossilized yellowish-brown resin that comes from ancient trees. It can be used for jewelry and ornaments.

carpenter A skilled craftsperson who makes objects from wood.

chlorophyll The green pigment in plants that traps the action of sunlight. Photosynthesis occurs, and food is produced for the plant.

coppicing The practice of cutting the trunks of woodland trees close to the ground to encourage the fast growth of shoots.

deciduous Trees that shed leaves each year in autumn.

ecosystem The group of animals and plants living in their environment.

environment The surroundings in which a plant or animal lives.

flexible Able to bend without breaking.

flora and fauna The plant and animal life of a particular place.

foliage The green parts of a plant.

food chain A community of living things dependent upon each other for food. Each feeds upon the species below in the chain.

grain The direction of the fibers in wood.

hardwoods Broad-leaved trees that have strong heavy wood, rather than the softwood produced by conifers.

horizontal Level or flat, parallel with the horizon.

kapok Silky fibers used in mattresses, life preservers, sleeping bags, and insulation.

knot A lump of plant tissue found on a tree, usually where a branch grew.

organic Relating to living things.

papier-mâché A hard substance made from a pulp of paper and paste.

resonant A material that amplifies sound vibrations passing through it because it vibrates as a result.

sap The watery food circulating inside a plant.

sapling A young tree.

seasoned wood Wood that has been dried to make it suitable for use by a carpenter.

softwoods Coniferous trees with open-grained wood.

tissue Animal or plant cells of the same kind.

vertical At right angles to the horizon— or upright.

More Information

Further Reading

Aldis, Rodney. *Rainforests.* Ecology Watch. New York: Dillon Press, 1991.

Burnie, David. *Tree.* Eyewitness Books. New York: Alfred Knopf Books for Young Readers, 1988.

Dowden, Anne O. *Blossom on the Bough: A Book of Trees.* New York: Ticknor & Fields Books for Young Readers, 1994.

Hirschi, Ron. *Save Our Forests.* A One Earth National Audubon Society Book. New York: Delacorte Press, 1993.

Javna, John. *Fifty Simple Things Kids Can Do to Save the Earth.* Kansas City, MO: Andrews & McMeel, 1990.

Stocks, Sue. *Collage.* First Arts and Crafts. New York: Thomson Learning, 1994.

Addresses for Information

Center for Marine Conservation
1725 Desales Street NW, Suite 500
Washington, DC 20036

Environmental Protection Agency
Public Information Center
Washington, DC 20460

Environmental Defense Fund
257 Park Avenue South
New York, NY 10010

Friends of the Earth
218 D Street SE
Washington, DC 20003

Greenpeace
1436 U Street NW
Washington, DC 20009

National Wildlife Federation
1400 16th Street NW
Washington, DC 20036

The Nature Conservancy
1436 North Lynn Street
Arlington, VA 22209

Rainforest Action Network
300 Broadway, Suite 28
San Francisco, CA 94133

You can also enroll in the Adopt-a-Forest program by writing to:
National Audubon Society
Washington State Office
P. O. Box 462
Olympia, WA 98507

Index